WRITING THE DASH
Drawing Inspiration from Life

**Enhance Your Writing and
Connect with Your Readers**

Linda Apple

Copyright © 2024 – Linda C. Apple
All cover art copyright © 2024 – Linda C. Apple
All Rights Reserved

No part of this book may be reproduced or transmitted in any form or by any means, electronic or mechanical, including photocopying, recording, or by any information storage and retrieval system, without permission in writing from the author.

Executive Editor – Clarissa Willis
Book Design – Sharon Kizziah-Holmes
Published by

SOLANDER
PRESS

Rogers, Arkansas

ISBN -13: 978-1-959548-36-2

Dedication

I dedicate this book to Lois Spoon, Velda Brotherton, and Dusty Richards. These mentors introduced me to the wonderful world of writing and taught me skills from the deep wealth of their knowledge. I will always be grateful for them.

CONTENTS

Dedication
The Dash 1
Knowing Your Authentic Self as a Writer 3
Finding Your Story 12
The Art of Writing 25
Memoir Writing 76
Furthermore 90
The End…Or Is It 94
About the Author 96

The Dash

The Dash between your birth date and death date is where life happens.

Inside each of us is a treasure, a wealth of experiences, lessons learned, wisdom gained, moments of clarity, laughter, and tears. None of these experiences—good times or hard times—should go to waste.

No matter what genre we write, fiction or nonfiction, we can draw from a deep well of our lives to create relatable and engaging prose for our readers. Why is this important? When we write from the perspectives and epiphanies we've gleaned, we give readers more than a wonderful story, more than an escape. One of my favorite C.S. Lewis quotes is, *"You too? I thought I was the only one."* So many of us have felt that same way. Isolation that holds us in a state of inertia. However, when we read a well-written piece and identify with it, we realize, like Lewis, that we are not alone. We may feel validated. We may realize there is a way out after all. We are reminded there is hope.

Writing the Dash, Drawing Inspiration from Life, will enhance your writing skills. Your prose will not only deeply connect with your readers but also convey the important message, "You are not alone."

~ Linda Apple

KNOWING YOUR AUTHENTIC SELF AS A WRITER

It is Wisdom to know others. It is enlightenment to know oneself. ~ Laozi

Recognize your core values. When I first began writing, I was all over the writing map. I tried to write like this author and then that author. I followed the trends, only to find they were already outdated. I listened to speakers who told me how to write, and I tried to do everything they said, even when one speaker contradicted the other. I dreamed of being famous, making big money, and being in demand. But reality kept slapping me in the face, making me want to quit. But, as many of you reading this book know, we can't stop writing.

Have you ever had an epiphany? When it feels as if the heavens open and light beams down with a special delivery message? Okay, that might be a little dramatic, but that is what it felt like when I attended the Ozark Creative Writers conference in the late 1990's. I had a magnificent epiphany. Page Lambert, author of *In Search of Kinship*, was one of the keynote speakers. In her presentation, she spoke one sentence illuminating my purpose as a writer. She said, "I cannot change the pain of my past, but I can give health to the future."

That statement resonated deep inside my soul. It probably didn't affect anyone else in that room, but it transformed me. Why? Because it spoke to my core values.

Core values—your personal values— are a collection of beliefs and opinions that define your standards of behavior. They guide your decision-making, shape your disposition, and influence your interactions with people around you. Core values are unique to each individual and are often established early in life. For instance, two of my core values is fostering creativity and encouraging others. Even as a child, I was a big idea person, always cheering on my friends.

Over the years, my core values have evolved and become more refined. Today, I know how to leverage them to enhance my writing and everything else I do. You may wonder, *is it necessary for me to know myself to write great stories?* No. However, if you want to impact your readers with your strengths, making them emotionally healthier after reading your work, then the answer is yes. When we write with the strength of our core values, we can make a positive difference in the lives of others. Always keep in mind the ripple effect. It isn't just our readers who are deeply touched. They, in turn, may make life better for those in their sphere of influence.

Realizing your core values strengthens your unique writing voice and forms a foundation crucial to your best writing. Although learning from other writers' styles is helpful, we must be mindful not to become mere imitations of them. To quote Judy Garland, "Always be a first-rate version of yourself instead of a second-rate version of somebody else."

In this chapter, there is a list of core values and an exercise to help determine which ones align with you. Your goal is to have a revelation of who you are, to embrace your values, and to infuse them in every part of your life, including your writing. This list isn't exhaustive. But it will jump-start you in discovering your core values. Others will soon present themselves.

CORE VALUE EXERCISE

Step 1:

Circle every word in the list that resonates with you. Move quickly, and don't analyze or overthink. Circle as many as you want.

Acceptance	**Accuracy**
Accountability	**Accuracy**
Achievement	**Adventure**
Advocacy	**Affirmation**
Appreciation	**Authority**
Autonomy	**Balance**
Benevolence	**Boldness**
Calmness	**Caring**
Challenge	**Change**
Charity	**Cheerfulness**
Comfort	**Community**
Commitment	**Compassion**
Collaboration	**Consistency**
Cooperation	**Cooperation**

Courtesy	**Creativity**
Credibility	**Daring**
Decisiveness	**Dedication**
Dependability	**Diversity**
Duty	**Empathy**
Encouragement	**Encouragement**
Excellence	**Fairness**
Faithfulness	**Family**
Fitness	**Flexibility**
Forgiveness	**Friendship**
Freedom	**Fun**
Generosity	**Genuineness**
Growth	**Health**
Honesty	**Hope**
Humility	**Humor**
Independence	**Individuality**
Innovation	**Individuality**
Inspiration	**Intelligence**
Intuition	**Joy**

Justice	Kindness
Knowledge	Leadership
Learning	Love
Loyalty	Impact
Mindfulness	Motivation
Openness	Mindedness
Optimism	Order
Passion	Perfection
Performance	Peace
Philanthropy	Power
Proactive	Professionalism
Purpose	Punctuality
Rationality	Recognition
Relationships	Reliability
Resilience	Risk
Safety	Security
Self-Control	Self-Esteem
Knowledge	Service
Simplicity	Solitude

Spirituality	**Stability**
Success	**Teamwork**
Thankfulness	**Thoughtfulness**
Tolerance	**Tradition**
Trustworthy	**Understanding**
Uniqueness	**Validation**
Versatility	**Vision**
Virtue	**Wealth**
Well-Being	**Wisdom**
Wonder	**Zeal**

Step 2:

You might have noticed that several of the values you circled are similar. That's good. Recognizing these common values will give you a more comprehensive understanding of their significance. Examine the words you circled and note those with similar meanings or attributes. Arrange them into groups based on their similarities. This is important. For instance, if one of your core values is wealth, you may fear this makes you sound materialistic. But philanthropy can also be grouped with wealth, which gives an excellent segue into many topics.

Step 3:

Within each group, rank each value based on its importance to you. These are your top core values.

Understanding your values can significantly elevate your writing and establish a deeper connection with your readers, whether you are writing fiction, non-fiction, essays, or poetry.

In my case, values such as inspiration, validation, encouragement, education, humor, and kindness are woven into everything I write. My desire is to entertain and empower my readers, offering encouragement, guidance, hope, and even lightening their burdens with a good belly laugh!

NOTES

FINDING YOUR STORY

A human being is nothing but a story with skin around it. ~ Fred Allen

Our dash is the weaving of moments, experiences, lessons, successes, failures, happiness, and fear. We have laughed, cried, loved, worked, played, and faced hardships. These compose the fabric of our life story.

Some people are natural storytellers, sharing their embellished anecdotes with ease. However, most do not recognize or appreciate the value of their life stories. The demands of survival often overshadow the narrative. Yet, we must not lose hope. Our stories are still there, waiting to be woven into the tapestry of humanity. We just need to uncover them and begin the process. This chapter contains exercises to help you discover your invaluable stories waiting to be told.

Life Landscapes

I mentioned in the first chapter about hearing Page Lambert speak. During her session she shared her insights on how the landscape of our lives shape who we are, what we do, and how we think. During her talk, Lambert gave us an exercise to help us rediscover forgotten memories and connect with our life's landscape. She encouraged us to choose a person from our life, living or deceased, and freewrite about them.

Freewriting is a technique that involves brainstorming on paper or a computer screen. It helps open the floodgates of your memories and creative ideas. During Page's session, I selected my grandmother, Molly Lowe, whom I affectionately called Mammie. (As a side note, never let your grandchildren name you.) When Page began the timer, I began to write. Here is a portion of what I wrote:

Adored me, walked a million miles with me in the zoo bought my first banana split. I miss her rode the bus with her to work Krystal hamburgers I could go for one of those right now beautiful gardens played in the yard sprinklr grew mint, had tea parties under the magnolia tree...

From this, one of the topics I highlighted was about tea parties. Several months later, I wrote a story about our parties under the magnolia tree and sold it to Chicken Soup for the Soul.

FREEWRITING EXERCISE

In this exercise, pick someone who has significantly impacted your life. Let your thoughts flow freely without concern for grammar, spelling, or maintaining a cohesive narrative. Just let them spill out.

Write continuously for 10-20 minutes without stopping. If you get stuck, write "I'm stuck" repeatedly until something else comes to mind. No matter if the thoughts have nothing to do with your subject. If something such as, *I could go for an ice cream sundae right now,* comes to mind, write it down. If you are freewriting on the computer, turn the screen away from you because if you watch the words on the screen, the temptation to edit is distracting.

Once you've finished freewriting, take a moment to read what you've written and highlight what stands out. You'll be surprised at the memories that surface and the new topics you may discover. Sometimes, it's just a single word that can open a whole new world of ideas. Don't throw what you wrote away. File it back and revisit it on occasion. New ideas may surface. Give it a try. Freewriting works for all topics. In addition to its other benefits, it is also quite cathartic.

NOTES

Daydream

Contrary to the notion that daydreaming is a waste of time, this isn't the case for a writer. Mental wandering, aptly called *wool-gathering by my grandfather,* is a valuable tool. When writers stare off in the distance, they are actively engaged in their creative process.

DAYDREAMING EXERCISE

Have a pen and paper with you and set aside at least 30 minutes. An hour is even better. Let your mind wander. Ask yourself, "What if...?" Unlike freewriting, you may only think of one word or one topic. That's okay. As I mentioned, it is hard to eliminate the feeling that you are wasting time. You're not. The most unexpected stories can emerge from these random musings, as well as a fresh perspective.

Notice everything around you, the scents, nature, light, people, and sounds, and let them tell you stories. Take notes and jot down your thoughts, no matter how small. Capture fleeting ideas before they disappear. Believe me, they vanish almost as instantly as they come.

I usually set my ramblings aside for a day or so and return to them. I find that some of the ideas are just *meh*. And others are, *Wow! Fantastic!*

NOTES

Write the Mundane

Whenever I teach a class on memoir writing, one question always comes up: "Why would anyone want to read about me? I'm just an ordinary person who hasn't accomplished anything noteworthy or experienced great adventures." However, this viewpoint can be a good thing because it means you have a vast audience of people who can relate to you. The only issue is that most individuals don't appreciate the value of their own stories.

My first attempt at a historical novel was set in 1850. To help me with authentic dialogue, my father gave me my great-grandfather's daily planner from 1874. This little 3x5 book contained a few jotted lines each day. One of his earliest entries, dated January 3, 1874, he wrote, *Mr. Kerr and myself went to sit up with Andrew tonight.* I wondered why. I continued to read and learned that Andrew was sick. Still, why did they sit with him? Was he alone? Were they giving his wife a much-needed rest? I also noted how he referred to himself as *myself.* I learned that he made his living growing cotton, how he ginned all summer and even hauled cottonseed on Christmas Eve, of all days. He helped build houses, barns, and chicken coops for his neighbors. One entry was about him having to go into town and appear in court. I wondered what kind of devilment he'd gotten himself into. I also read about his budding relationship with Dr. Webb's daughter, Mary, who later became my great-grandmother. All of this fascinated me. It was like reaching back in time and meeting him. Although he had only jotted down a year's worth of daily life, I was immersed. I read it like I ate potato chips, unable to stop at one page. Holding something that my great-grandfather had held in the late 1800s was nothing short of magical. If I could go back in time and tell him how much I treasure this planner, he'd probably laugh. Yet it is true. As time passes, even the mundane becomes compelling to people decades later.

If you think about it, the ordinary tapestry of everyday life gives us a profound connection to our ancestors. A rich narrative unfolds that transcends time and culture. When we write what we consider mundane life, we are offering more than we realize to those who come after us. Much like a beam of light traveling through a prism, our personal stories cast a shower of color, unexpectedly illuminating paths for others.

Never underestimate the worth of your stories. Instead, think of them as your enduring legacy, your contribution to your readers now and future generations.

Be Observant

Drawing inspiration from life requires you to open your eyes to the world around you. Responsibilities, challenges, and the people relying on us often tether our focus to survival, causing us to miss the brilliant life unfolding around us. Do yourself a favor. Look up.

Notice what is around you even if you only have twenty minutes of downtime. Be curious. For instance, when I'm outside, I like to observe and learn in nature's classroom.

One spring morning, I watched sparrows checking out all the ferns that hung from the porch eves. It was as if they were house hunting. A lot of discussion went on among them. However, a pair of wrens were ahead of the real estate rush. They had found the perfect spot to build their home and raise their young—the covered barbeque grill. If you think about it, that would make an ideal spot. It was covered, protecting the nest from rain. They entered through the vent close to the bottom. The hole was too small for a hawk or cat to invade. Yet, there was an unknown danger the little wrens couldn't comprehend. Fire. Even though their nests were continually removed, the determined birds soldiered on. Finally, the only way to keep them out was to close the vent.

I reflected on the wrens' dilemma and how

something always messed with their nests. A thought occurred to me. Life sometimes messed with my nest, which required me to go in another direction, and it usually turned out to be better. When I went back inside, I wrote a devotional based on the story of the wrens. Like the little birds, we think we know what is best, but our lack of understanding might lead us to harm. I hoped to encourage my readers not to be disheartened when their plans were frustrated. Sometimes, detours led to better outcomes. Above all, it was a gentle reminder for them to never give up and always be open to finding another way.

Another lesson I learned from observation came when I noticed a tiny cucumber plant defiantly growing in the middle of the gravel road between our house and the garden. It must have fallen from the packet when I walked to the garden. In the dust from crushed rocks, a minuscule leaf the size of the end of my thumb and a pinhead-size bloom emerged. Closer inspection revealed a thread-like stem and a cucumber the size of a grain of rice.

I marveled at this tenacious plant defying the odds. Its brave persistence accomplished its destined purpose to yield fruit. My observation? Never give up, even when the odds are against me. I wanted to be like that cucumber plant. I blogged about my epiphany. The last line said it all, *"This little plant didn't feed my body. It accomplished something much greater. It fed my soul."*

We have an idea of how things should be, but there might be something greater if we don't give up.

The more you practice observation, you will have not only more topics to write about, but also a richer life.

Your Final Word

Reflect upon the legacy you wish to leave for others to draw inspiration from after you leave this earth. What do you consider essential for your readers to grasp? Write it down. Never underestimate the value of your work. Your words can create a lasting impact and motivate generations to come.

THE ART OF WRITING

*The true alchemists do not change lead into gold;
they change the world into words.
~ William H. Gass*

During a recent conversation with a young writer, he expressed the desire to write fiction based on his personal experiences. His goal was to offer readers a window into his perspective in order to help them understand individuals with the same background as his. Of course, I highly encouraged him to move ahead with his writing aspiration. Then he asked if college was a requirement to pursue a career in writing. I assured him that he didn't need to go to college but explained there were elements he'd need to learn to connect with readers and keep them engaged.

In this chapter, I will cover those basic elements that every writer needs to begin. Even established writers can benefit from a refresher on these basics. These fundamental components are necessary for good fiction. However, they are also excellent to use in nonfiction as well. This style of writing is known as Creative Nonfiction, which we will delve into in the next chapter.

THE EIGHT FUNDAMENTAL WRITING COMPONENTS

PLOT

Some wonder what the first step is in writing their story, plot, or characterization. My answer? Yes. It is up to you. If your inspiration begins with a certain storyline, go with it and add the characters who will carry that storyline to its finish. If you have a character in mind, write a plot that will make your protagonist drive the story.

You may be asked, "Are you a pantser or a plotter?" What they are asking is, do you write by the seat of your pants and let the story come to you and develop as you go? Or do you have a story in mind, and you outline the storyline? I'm sort of both. I usually have an idea in mind and allow my characters to introduce themselves and their narrative to me. You decide. It is your story.

No matter what you begin with, plot or character, you must know what makes a strong and interesting plot. Let's look at six elements of plot.

In the Beginning:

Exposition
Here, you introduce your main characters and their world. You briefly describe settings and their

normal life situation, but also a dream they hold, a goal, or a desire. This is necessary for your reader to understand what went wrong when you go to the next element.

Think of EB White's book, *Charlotte's Web*. The exposition introduces Fern at the breakfast table with her father, who tells her his plan to kill a runt pig. A horrified Fern convinces him to let her have the piglet. She names the pig, Wilber, and treats him like one of her baby dolls. Her father sells the pig to another farmer. Wilber misses Fern but befriends a spider named Charlotte.

Now, we are introduced to Wilber's world.

Inciting Element

After you have briefly established the "norm" for your character and his or her goal, you now put your protagonist in an abnormal circumstance out of his or her comfort zone, an unmet desire. This is the beginning of the tension that will drive your story forward. It throws your character into an upsetting or challenging situation out of his or her control. What this inciting element is depends on your genre. Consider what should go wrong, becoming a roadblock on your character's way to happiness or victory.

Wilber's conflict begins when he learns the farmer is fattening him up because he was to become the main course at Christmas dinner. Of course, he doesn't want to die.

During the Middle:

Rising Action

This is the bulk of your story or book. Your storyline is moving toward its culmination. Your main characters are moving toward their goal only to be frustrated by complications and obstructions that keep them from reaching it. Just as they are about to succeed, you throw in a curve. Your reader will be wholly engrossed, turning the pages to discover what happens.

The spider, Charlotte, comes up with a plan to weave messages about Wilber in her web. The farmer is impressed and tells everyone to come and see Charlotte's web.

Charlotte continues to weave messages, inspiring the farmer to take Wilber to the fair. Charlotte, although tired and in desperate need to build her egg sac, agrees to go.

At the End:

Climax

At this point, you've built tension. Your reader is invested in your main character and, hopefully, is on the edge, wanting a successful outcome. Give it to them. They've earned it.

Wilber wins a special prize at the fair for being

"out of the ordinary." He is now safe. But Charlotte has grown old and tired. Wilber wants her to come back to the farm, but she is too weak. So, he takes her egg sac back with him.

Resolution
You wrap up all the loose ends in this last portion of your narrative. Your characters are now in their "new" normal. They have either reached their goal or the goal has changed. It is important that your characters have also changed in some way from when the story first started.

Wilber returns and is welcomed home with enthusiasm. He puts Charlotte's egg sac in the barn and waits for them to hatch. When they finally do, Wilber is sad to see how they let out their fine silk threads and float away. However, three choose to stay with him and are good friends. Wilber lives to see generations of Charlotte's progeny.

Suggestion: If you intend to write a series, this is a good place to slip in another conflict or a question to be answered in the next book.

POINT OF VIEW

Point of View, or POV, is important to the development of the plot and characterization because it tells the reader which character or narrator is telling the story. It can be told from their perspective in four main ways:
- **1st Person POV** — uses "I" and "we"
- **2nd Person POV** — uses "you"
- **3rd Person POV** — uses "she" "he" "they" and "it"

Point of view strengthens your writing because it clarifies the story and keeps it consistent. Think of it as entering the physical and mental being of your character.

Each POV offers a unique approach.

1st Person – This perspective gives the closest and most personal insight into your character. Readers experience what your character knows. They observe the same sights and sense the physical and emotions of the character. Because your character has limited access to information, you can build powerful suspense.

1st person narration—this is the character who is telling the story, speaking about only the things the character can experience through his or her senses, emotions, and personal thoughts. The character cannot know what others are thinking or doing out of sight.

2ⁿᵈ Person — The second-person perspective is an odd POV that uses the unspoken "me" to speak to "you." A line in a story might go something like this: *You walked into the house and sunk low in the chair. The phone rang, and you answered it, not really wanting to talk.*

This POV is rarely used in literature but is popular in short creative works.

3ʳᵈ Person — While first person is writing from an inside perspective, (I, you), and directly addresses the reader, third person is telling the story from an *outside* perspective, (he, she, we, they). And doesn't directly address the reader. The author is the narrator telling the story but from the main character's perspective. The beauty of third person is that the narrator can describe what is happening with multiple characters, describing their thoughts and feelings.

3ʳᵈ person can be broken into two more categories:

3ʳᵈ Person Limited — Here is where the narrator can only see into one character's mind per scene. For example, JK Rowling told Harry Potter's story through Harry Potter's perspective. We could only see, hear, smell, taste, feel, or think what he could. We couldn't know these things about Ron unless he told the other characters in the story about them.

You can take this further and write what is called "deep POV." This is considered an "immersive POV," which is one step deeper into the main character. You do not need to use defining words such as saw, watched, thought, or felt.

The following sentence is 3rd person in Jessie's POV.

Jessie waited for the announcement. He wondered if he would win the contest as he watched the contest chair approach the microphone.

Following is Jessie's immersive POV:

Jesse waited for the announcement. Would he finally win a contest? The Contest chair approached the microphone.

See how it has the feel of you stepping into Jesse and experiencing the scene exactly as he does? Deep POV is succinct writing and eliminates the need for dialogue tags and unnecessary adverbs. Think of it as using the character's voice instead of the narrator's bringing the character closer to the reader and cutting out the middleman.

There is the temptation when writing in 3rd person to "head hop." This means the point of view changes from one character to another within the same scene. This is frowned on by most publishers.

You can use multiple POVs, but to ensure readers do not get confused, define the POV switches by moving them into another scene and introducing them by name at the beginning of that scene in order for the readers to follow the story. For example, in my book, *Avalee's Gift,* Avalee breaks down in front of her friend Lexi about a problem she cannot overcome. After Lexi comforts Avalee, she leaves the house. Lexi is now the main character in the next scene, and the first sentence introduces her by name, for example, *Lexi paced in her office, trying to come up with a solution.*

If you are a beginning writer, it is best to stick with one or two POV characters in a chapter.

3rd Person Omniscient — in this POV, the narrator is god-like in that everything is known about every character. What they are thinking, seeing, feeling. The narrator knows everything about all the characters, their stories, thoughts, feelings, what is happening in every room, and every setting, as well as their backstory and future events.

CHARACTER DEVELOPMENT

When writing a novel, your characters become real to you, or at least they should. This holds true even for short stories and essays. At the first meeting with your characters, you may think you know everything about them. However, as you write, you may find there are gaps in your understanding of them, causing you to either come to a standstill in your story or, even worse, all causing your characters to sound the same.

There are many opinions on characterization, and everything I've heard or read is good advice. After years of writing, I've devised a technique that works for me. The same will be true for you. When you read or hear the many ways of character development, choose what resonates with you and what aligns with your creative instincts and style.

In this section, I will share my approach to building my characters. Before starting this process, I make a file on each one describing their physical features, age, birth date, personality, strengths, challenges, childhood, and background, including information on parents and sometimes even grandparents. This helps when I want to check and ensure I'm on target. I may not use everything in my file, but it helps me know them individually and keep from blending them together. The following is the method I use to build my characters.

Motivation and/or Goals

The characters need a goal to get the story started. If you think back to your favorite novels, you will be able to identify these. For instance, in *The Lord of the Rings,* Frodo is an ordinary hobbit living among his family and friends. What sets him apart is his incorruptible heart. He is given the responsibility to take a ring that wields the incredible power of temptation, cast it into the fire of Mordor, and destroy it. Another example is Jo in *Little Women.* She wants to be a great writer.

Both examples illustrate what is commonly called a "story arc," which represents the internal change the character goes through in your story. He or she will not be the same at the end as in the beginning. The character must overcome time and time again to reach his or her goal. The goal may change as well, as in Jo, whose goal changed from being a great writer to opening a school accessible to any child, no matter his or her social status. Frodo's goal did not change. He accomplished it, but his life was changed.

Physical Appearance and Personality Profile

I put these together because I had to have an idea of their personalities before I could envision them. My first novel, *Women of Washington Avenue,* is about four friends who are too old to be young but too young to be old, and they all find romance again. I knew all four would be Southern ladies, but I didn't know what they would look like until I knew their personalities. I had daydreamed about the plot and knew that Avalee was a successful designer who had escaped to New York after a tragedy. She returned to Moonlight to help her widowed mother, who was about to lose the family business. Lexi, a local journalist whose husband cheated on her with a minor and wound up in prison, is a spitfire whose bitterness manifests in sarcasm. Molly Kate is a plus-sized baker who is sick of body shaming and flaunts her curves with pride. And finally, Jema, the kind, empathetic, and gentle volunteer.

Their personality profile was far from finished, but I had enough to go on to describe what they looked like. I researched images on the Internet and actresses who had similar personalities in some of the roles they played. After choosing the perfect match, I saved a picture of each and put it in the characters file.

Now, it was time to go deeper into each lady's personality traits. The first thing I did was write their history. I know this sounds like a lot, but trust me, you will not only understand what drives your character, you will also use some of it throughout the book, and if your book is part of a series, you will probably use it then as well.

For Avalee, I went back two generations because of her storyline about the family business. But for the others, I made a historical record of where they were born and the date. I named their parents and wrote about their childhood and teen years. I wrote about their school, friends, first husbands, and their children.

After I finished their history, I delved deeper. I wondered about their secrets, their insecurities, and their hidden pain. I also thought about their strengths, talents, favorite things to eat, favorite colors, fashion style, and how they decorated. What were their hobbies? Favorite time of year? Taste in men?

Finally, I assigned them a personality. This is something I came up with, and I love it. I gave each one an element from nature: fire, air (wind), earth, and *water*. I've studied a lot of personality profiles. I've even taught them, but the profile using the elements is my favorite because it is visual and easy to remember. All you have to do is visualize the attributes of each element, both positive and negative. Fire gives light but also depletes oxygen. Air lifts things up. Think of a kite. However, when out of control, it can also blow you away. Earth gives stability and nurtures but can also be smothering. Water is supportive and reflective, but it also floods.

When you assign an element to each character, it

will keep you from melding one into another. You will know how they respond and react, as well as what they will do in a crisis. Knowing their element reveals how they will interact with another person. For instance, when a fire person and a water person are together and the fire person gets too intense, the water person can either cool the situation down, or put the fire person out completely. When fire and wind argue, if wind blows on fire, the fire grows hotter. The fire person can suck out all wind's oxygen. The earth person is creative. Think of all the beauty that comes from the earth. Wind can scatter seeds, and water can moisten the ground. Get the idea?

After you've assigned an element or two for each character, note it in each character's file. As you write, your character will reveal more. Hearing our characters speak to us is a mystical experience exclusive to writers. That's probably why we love getting together at conferences. If we talk about it to others, they think we are odd. The first time this happened to me was while writing my first historical novel (which has been laid to rest in a drawer). I named my heroine Sadie. No matter how much I tried to get to know her, I couldn't figure her out at all. Then, one afternoon, while driving to the grocery store, in my mind, I heard, "My name is Elizabeth." When I returned home, I changed her name, and the novel flowed. Well, at least I thought it did. Publishers, not so much.

For your secondary characters, their backstory isn't as important to know right away. If needed, it will come to you. But to know their personality and appearance is necessary to understand and write their dynamics with other characters.

For more ideas for element traits, visit my website, lindaapple.com, and click the materials tab.

PERSONALITY ELEMENTS EXERCISE

- Give each element, fire, air, earth, water, its own page.
- Write all you can think of listing:
  - what the element looks like
  - What it feels like
  - What it smells like
  - What it sounds like
  - How it helps us
  - How it hurts us
  - How each interacts with the others
- Now, write the names of people who remind you of that element and why.

NOTES

NOTES

SCENE AND SEQUEL

Scene and sequel advance the plot of the story. The scene moves the story forward as your character tries to achieve a goal. The sequel shows the character's reaction to the scene where they analyze their situation and then decide on their plan of action.

I once heard a scene and sequel compared to a train. Your story or book is a line of scenes and sequels. The scenes are the railroad cars and sequels are the coupler joining them together. The scene is your character's action, and the sequel is the reaction.

Each scene follows a pattern:
1. **Goal** – What your character wants.
2. **Conflict** – the obstacles that keep them from the goal.
3. **Outcome** – the dilemma that comes from the conflict.

Author Dwight V. Swain, in his book *Techniques of the Selling Writer*, labels the third (Outcome) as Disaster. Only, I find that a bit extreme, given what most consider a disaster.

Let's look at an example in the Anne of Green Gables novel. In chapter 27, *Vanity and Vexation of Spirit,* Anne has a **goal:** to have Raven-black hair. Her **dilemma**: she has red hair—which she despises. The **outcome,** or in this case, Swain's word is appropriate, is a **disaster:** she winds up with an odd shade of bronzy green hair with some of her natural red streaks mixed in.

This leads us to the sequel, which follows the pattern:
1. **Reaction** – emotional follow through
2. **Dilemma** – trying to know what to do.
3. **Decision** – the character makes a choice.

Anne's **reaction:** utter despair. Her **dilemma:** not being able to turn her hair back to her natural color. Her **decision:** letting Marilla cut her hair.

A word of advice: only add to the scene what "defines" the scene. In the scene about Anne dying her hair, it would be distracting to write about a long conversation over breakfast with Marilla about making fig preserves. However, if they chatted about how she hated her red hair, that would fit the scene.

How many scenes should you have per chapter or in short works? Two at the most is recommended. However, the choice is up to you, the writer. Just ensure your writing doesn't jump track and confuse the reader. Keep your scenes and sequels on a smooth course to the end.

SENSE OF PLACE

This is one of my favorite elements of writing. Sense of place plunges your readers into the heart of your prose. Let's explore how using the five senses in your prose can captivate readers in your narrative.

Using the Five Senses

Using the senses is a powerful writing tool. Incorporating sight, sound, taste, touch, and smell are keys that open your readers' minds and memories, creating a strong connection point. Their evoked memories add an even deeper description that they unconsciously weave into the words you wrote. This is especially useful when writing short stories and essays where word count constraints limit elaborate descriptions.

If you haven't already heard the writing mantra, *show, don't tell,* you will. The senses will aid you in showing. Using them effectively is better than a string of over-used adjectives. Such as *the loud call of the blue jays* or *the sour taste of the lemon.* Your readers are familiar with the words loud and sour and will skim over them. We want our readers to hear the jay's shards of broken glass calls and to *taste* the lemon's acidic juice, smell the summer freshness on its skin, and feel the tingles that run from your jaw to your ear.

To ensure my readers connected with my scenes, I came up with an exercise I call the *Five Sense Refresher* to keep me from depending on tired adjectives. I do this often, especially when I feel my writing is plodding along. At the end of this section, I have included an exercise to help you get started.

Sound – When I want to refresh myself on sound, I either go outside or someplace public, like a coffee shop. I close my eyes and listen, only opening them long enough to jot down what I hear. After a while, I freewrite about the sounds and use metaphors—something that is not literally applicable but suggests a resemblance. One morning a flock of jays gathered in a tree close by and as I mentioned earlier, I compared their annoying sound to shards of broken glass. Poor blue jays. They must have been at the end of the line when bird calls were handed out.

Taste – I choose a few things at a time to taste. Something salty, sweet, sour, bitter, spicy, creamy, crunch, hot, cold, you get the idea. I take a bite or a sip and hold it in my mouth. I record any physical reaction, emotional reaction, how it feels on my tongue, and what comes to my mind, such as comparisons, opinions, or memories. Then, I describe it metaphorically, physically, and emotionally.

Have you ever thought about how we don't always taste by putting something in our mouths? I discovered this while visiting the ocean. I tasted salt just breathing in the briny air.

Smell – To me, smell is akin to time travel. A familiar aroma can take me back in time. Once, while visiting an elderly church member, the moment I stepped inside her house, in my mind, I immediately went back to my late grandmother's home. The aroma of lemon polish mingled with freshly brewed coffee enveloped me. Something on the stove simmered, releasing an aroma with the faintest hint of freshly mown grass and hickory smoke. I knew right away green beans and ham hock were in the pot because that is how it smelled in my grandmother's kitchen. Instantly, I was there in her house. My throat tightened, and my eyes burned. As the kind lady poured our coffee, I excused myself from the kitchen and went to another room to wipe away the tears, demanding release. Bleach takes me back to swimming in a pool on a hot summer day when I was a child. The warm, spicy scent of cinnamon plops me in a comfy chair where I watch a roaring fire during winter.

Touch – There are countless textures around us, ranging from fabrics, plants, and animals to people, stone, wood, and more. When you refresh your senses through touch, notice how your fingertips, palms, and feet may perceive textures in different, distinct ways.

Notice what touches you. In the South, the air is sometimes muggy and heavy, like a wet blanket thrown over your head. But when I'm hot and sweaty, a muggy breeze cools me. On a balmy evening, I relish the gentle, velvety caress of a cool breeze against my face but not the tickle of a wayward hair on my cheek.

Sight – In my opinion, this is the easiest sense because we report what we see. It is also the sense writers use most and, with it, a long string of adjectives. The challenge for a writer is to discover things that have gone unnoticed in the past.

Years ago, I lived in a house near a school bus stop. Every day after school, a young boy would leave the bus and walk past my house on his way home. I noticed how he'd stop in front of my house each day and stare at the large oak tree in my yard. After a few minutes, he'd return to walking home.

I wondered what he saw in the tree. The next afternoon, I stretched out beneath the branches and gazed up. I anticipated the sight of grey bark heavy with green-lobed leaves. But what I saw surprised me. Even though I knew the leaves were all the same color, I saw many shades of green. Those close to the trunk were the color of a summer forest in the evening. The leaves illuminated by the sun were a pure Kelly green. Even though the leaves were the same green, the sun's light and the shadows created an illusion of different shades.

I continued watching all the life unfolding under the canopy. Birds swooped in and rested on branches, serenading with their songs. A mottled gray moth clung to the trunk, nearly blending in with the bark. Squirrels played a game of chase, causing acorns to tumble around me. Reclining beneath the tree, I thought about how often I merely glanced at the richness of life around me. I needed to be more childlike and more curious.

Light and shadow are excellent ways to create mood in your scene. A shadowy room where the only light is a lamppost outside the window sets the scene for sorrow, depression, or loneliness. A single candle flame within the room can indicate hope.

People's body language, facial expressions, and gestures give insight into their personalities and particular moments.

Describing a room gives insight into a character's personality and life situations. A gleaming desk where everything is orderly, including the perfectly aligned pen and paper, indicates a meticulous and disciplined person who sits there. What would a couch filled with mismatched pillows, magazines scattered on the floor, and mugs covering the coffee table tell you about the person who lived there?

See things differently. When Laura Ingalls' sister, Mary, became blind, their father asked Laura to be "Mary's eyes." Laura used inventive ways to help Mary become aware of her surroundings. Mary often asked Laura to "see it out loud for me, please." On their first train trip, Laura tried to tell Mary how fast the telegraph poles were going by. She said, "The wire sags down between them and swoops up again." Then she started counting them, "One—oop! Two—oop! Three! That's how fast they're going."

Laura used her voice, she used sound, to describe not only the sight but the motion as well. After I read that, I thought of ways to describe things differently than how we normally experience them. Not only did I have fun with it, but it also expanded my descriptions. I've included some ideas in the following exercise.

SENSES REFRESHER EXERCISE

Begin with freewriting – freewrite for two minutes about the sensations, thoughts, or memories that come to mind from the following list:

Snow	**Ice**
Christmas	**Mountains**
Clouds	**Rain**
Oceans	**Lakes**
Betrayal	**Past Loves**
Friends	**Loyalty**
Fear	**Loneliness**
Laughter	**Freedom**
Smoke	**Hearth fire**
Campfires	**Marshmallows**
Sweet	**Sour**
Spring	**Summer**
Autumn	**Winter**
Pets	**Hobbies**
Books	**Movie**

NOTES

Wake up your wonder – We use our senses every day and usually think nothing about them. Let's wake up our wonder. Choose from the list below and try to look beyond the physical. Immerse yourself in the wonder of it and write your observations.
- Pick a flower, smell its fragrance, inspect it.
- Study the night sky and let your thoughts flow.
- Examine your hands. They are used to communicate, work, create. We use them every day and only think about them when they hurt. Flex them, study them, and write what comes to mind.
- Touch nature, a warm stone, the tips of grass blades, rough tree bark, or the velvet of rose petals.

Heighten your senses –

- Close your eyes or obscure your vision in some way and listen. No matter where you are, in a coffee shop, the park, in a classroom, or at home. Freewrite what you hear and the memories that come to you.
- Taste from the following list and record your physical reaction to them, the memories evoked, and any other thoughts. Taste something:

Sweet	**Sour**
Bitter	**Spicy / Hot**
Creamy	**Crunchy**
Acidic	**Savory**

- Smell different spices in your spice cabinet. Describe them as if you are telling someone who has never had the sense of smell what the scent is like.
- Smell (very carefully) cleaning solutions in your home. What memories come to you?
- Go to a bakery or coffee shop and describe the aromas, the desires, and the memories that come to you.

I came up with this exercise after reading about how Laura Ingalls described things to her sister, Mary. This is fun to do when you get writer's brain fog. I'll get you started with a few ideas and then come up with your own.

Choose one sense from each or use all the ones suggested:
- Describe the sky using the senses of taste, touch, or smell.
- Describe the aroma of coffee by using the senses of touch or hearing.

- Describe rain using the senses of taste, hearing, or touch.
- Describe music using sight, touch, or taste.
- Pick a color and describe it using taste, smell, touch, and sound.
- Describe joy using all the senses.
- Describe fear using all the senses.
- Describe love using hearing, taste, or smell.
- Describe resentment using all the senses.
- Describe peace using all the senses.

Have fun awakening your senses to new and higher dimensions. No doubt your readers will wonder, *how did this writer come up with that? Fantastic!*

Never forget…you ARE fantastic!

DIALOGUE

Dialogue is an additional way for readers to get to know your characters by unveiling their personalities, temperaments, and their unique manner of speaking.

- **Character's Voice** —Variations in speech patterns come from factors such as education level, occupation, interests, social and economic status, and culture. Take these into account to guarantee each character stands out distinctly without blending with the others.
- **Be Real** — Words that flow from our fingertips are not necessarily the same as what comes from our mouths. For some reason, many of us tend to write dialogue more formally than how people actually speak, giving our prose a stilted feel. The characters speak *at* each other rather than *to* each other. As an example, consider the formal exchange between Janie and Robin speaking *at* each other:

Janie walked into Robin's corner office and said, "It is a beautiful day for a walk.

Robin replied, "I cannot go because I have a looming deadline on a project my boss said I must finish.
"But it is your lunch hour," said Janie. "You are entitled to that."
"Nonetheless," said Janie. "I have to work."

Is that how we talk to each other? Probably not. Their conversation would probably sound more like the following:

Janie strolled into Robin's office and smiled. "It's a beautiful day for a walk."
Robin looked up and sighed. "I can't. The boss is on my back about meeting my deadline."
"But it's your lunch hour.
"Doesn't matter." Robin rolled her shoulders. "I gotta finish."

See how natural that sounds. It is helpful to have someone read back to you what you wrote. You may find yourself scratching your head and thinking, *huh?*

To write dialogue that sounds natural, take the time to eavesdrop on the people and jot down what you hear. What filler words do they use? A woman who used to work for my husband ended every sentence with "You know." When my Southern relatives don't know how to answer, they always say, "There you go." What kind of slang or exclamations do people use? When my grandmother and her friends got together for neighborhood gossip and coffee, you could hear her either exclaim, "Mercy," or "I'll swan." I went to lunch with a very successful writer friend at a conference a few years ago. A perky waitress came to our table to take our order, all the while snapping her gum. When he ordered a chicken sandwich, she repeated, "One yard bird on a raft." My friend was fascinated and wrote that on a napkin, including the gum popping. I have no doubt she'll be in his next novel.

Pay attention to the cadence of their speech. What is the pace and the beat? Do they talk fast and run their sentences together? Do they drag out a one-syllable word into three?

Notice the different voice tones and inflections. Do they drawl, mumble, or do they clip their words? Does their voice carry all over the room, or is it whisper-soft? When you pay attention to the dialogue you hear around you every day, you will not only write believable dialogue, but you also have an additional characterization tool!

Show Dialogue — Once again, the writer's mantra, *show, don't tell,* is true. Along with the words that are spoken, the speaker will also use facial expressions and body language. I have a friend who always twirls a tendril of her hair when she speaks. I cannot speak without using my hands. My dad used to bob his head at the end of his sentence.

When writing a conversation between two characters breaking up, you may have one biting her lip and the other staring at the ground. A child may see her daddy walk through the door, throw her hands in the air, and shout, "You're home." A character may slap the table for emphasis while making his point. The businesswoman may stare over tented fingers while confronting her partner. Play out conversations on the screen of your mind and see your character's expressions and body language before writing.

Dialect — Use dialect like you use salt. Just enough to enhance the flavor. Too much dialect ruins dialogue, in the same way too much salt overpowers food. The constant use of dialect makes your story hard to read and fatiguing.

I use a few common Southern phrases, which are enough for my readers' brains to interpret the accent automatically. The same is true for any dialect you use for your story. Avoid "over salting" dialect.

The Correct Order in Dialogue — when writing a character's action and reaction, think about how this happens in real life. For instance, if I see a snake,

I'm startled, gasp, and then take a quick step back. There are two ways to write this. I can show the action first then the reaction or the reaction then the action. You decide which one is stronger.

She jumped back when she saw a snake, startled by it.

This sentence isn't grammatically incorrect. But it does imply that she wasn't startled until she stepped back. It is better to think about a real-life scenario:

Seeing a snake startled her, and she jumped back.

See how placing the reaction before the action strengthens the sentence? The same is true with dialogue. For example:

"Good morning," he said when he opened the door.
"He opened the door and said, "Good morning."

Again, both are correct, but the second sentence is stronger. When writing dialogue with actions, play the scene in your mind, and think about how it would actually happen.

Taper the Tags — Dialogue tags let the reader know which character is speaking, usually indicated simply by the word "said." However, when overused, tags are a distraction. Amateur writers use overblown tags like gasped, questioned, muttered, groaned, well, you get the idea. Nothing pulls me out of a story like superfluous dialogue tags. Following are three good rules of thumb for dialogue tags:

- **Formatting** – When there are only two characters in the scene, start a new paragraph each time the speaker changes. This way, your reader will be able to keep up with who is speaking.
- **Use an action** – When there are more than two people in the scene, show some kind of action to indicate who is speaking. For instance:

Lexi looked over the menu. "The crème Brule looks good."

"Yeah." Avalee laid her menu on the table. "But it won't look good on my thighs."

Molly Kate raised an eyebrow and smirked. "Honestly, Avalee, You are skin and bones as it is. You could use a few extra pounds."

- **Get Real** — Avoid using unrealistic verbs for attributive tags. They are not only annoying to the reader, but many are impossible. Take this line of dialogue, for example:

"I can't believe it, we won!" gasped Nancy.

Now, I want you to try and gasp that sentence.

It is much better to write:
Nancy gasped. "I can't believe it. We won!"

You showed an action, then the dialogue. The picture of her astonishment is the same, and the sentence is realistic.

Anytime you are tempted to use verbs such as groaned, growled, snarled, or chuckled, etc, as a sentence tag, try to do it yourself first and see how impossible it is. It's best to either rearrange your sentence to show an action, then the dialogue, as well as the character's facial expression, and body language.

Avoid the Obvious — Continually ending a sentence with qualifying tags is unnecessary and tiresome. If your character asks a question, there is no need to write, *"she asked."* The sentence has a question mark to let the reader know she asked.

Likewise, when a character tells another something, there is no need to use the tag *"he told her."* We read his telling her.

Avoid Adverbs After Tags — This is another annoying habit we writers sometimes fall into. Nothing makes readers feel as if they are slogging through knee-deep mud while they try to read a scene where the dialogue is peppered with adverbs used as tags. Read the following example:

"Richard is coming over." She announced happily.
"Who?" He replied loudly.
"You know, Richard, my friend from college." She answered brightly.
"Are you cheating on me?" He asked accusingly.
"You don't trust me." She replied mournfully.

Tedious, right? Also, notice the use of replied, answered, and asked. The readers understand without the writer telling them. It is much better to show, don't tell:

"Richard is coming over." She fisted her hands under her chin and bounced on her toes.
"Who?" He yelled over the blasting metal music.
She smiled and turned down the volume. "You know, Richard, my friend from college."

He lowered his brows and glared. "*Are you cheating on me?*"

Her mouth dropped open. "*Of course not. I can't believe you said that.*"

Written this way, the scene flows, and the reader can envision it.

Formatting Dialogue — The following are some tips for writing understandable dialogue:
- Keep all speech between quotation marks, including punctuation marks.
- If the same character talks long enough to require a new paragraph, place an opening quotation at the beginning of each paragraph but not a closing one at the end. When the character finishes speaking, place a closing quotation at the end of the last paragraph.
- When a character quotes another character within dialogue, use single quotes around the quote.

Fred laughed and said, "*I wished my uncle a merry Christmas, and he said, 'Bah Humbug.' I'm telling you the truth.*"

DIALOGUE EXERCISE

Getting It Right

I can't express this enough. Getting dialogue right is harder than most realize. If our four-year-old character sounds like a forty-year-old character, we have problems with our dialogue. If our wise old uncle sounds like a thirty-something corporate manager, we have missed the mark. If our drama-queen teen sounds like a grandma, well, you see how that just doesn't work.

Take the time to eavesdrop on conversations around you. Make note of:
- Voice tone, inflection, and sound.
- Notice the pace and beat. Fast? Do their words run together?
- Filler words, such as "you know," "so," etc.
- Unique phrases and expressions, such as, "there you go," "I'm slayed."
- Consistently mispronounced words. My mother used to say "alltimers" for Alzheimer's. My brother always said, "matter of factly," instead of "matter of fact."

Keep something with you to record dialogue elements. Consider it your "dialogue thesaurus!"

NOTES

INTERNALIZATION

This is also called *internal dialogue.* It is our character's inner voice, their stream of consciousness. Our readers are privy to the character's unspoken thoughts and feelings. They know what the character is struggling with and the reasoning behind their choices and decisions. Internalization is great for conflict.

Our character may say one thing but mean something else. It is useful for giving your readers hints of the past or information. However, it isn't a place for an information dump. Just a sentence or two here and there.

Internalization is also great for humor. The late Bobby Collins, a comedian, had a routine called "On the Inside." He would recount a confrontation he experienced, claiming how he boldly exclaimed his opinion or thoughts to the other person. Then, after a pause, he'd say, "On the inside." Then he'd meekly admit how he caved. Haven't we thought one thing but said another?

Inner dialogue is also the perfect place for reflective thought. It lends even more intimacy between your character and readers, as well as the opportunity to offer insight.

Formatting Internalization — When your character has inner thoughts, use italics. Only use quotation marks if the character is alone and thinking out loud.

EMOTION

If you think about it, we feel some kind of emotion several times each day. They affect and reflect our mental and physical well-being. When we write about our character's emotions, our readers will identify with them personally or with someone they know, helping them to relate to our story.

Every waking hour, and even in our dreams, we feel emotions. The same should be true for our characters. We want our readers to relate to their emotions, allowing them to identify with their emotional experiences. Through this connection, readers develop empathy with our protagonists and even, to some extent, have a touch of admiration mixed in with the aversion toward our antagonists.

But how much emotion should we add to keep it in balance and the story moving forward instead of slogging through drama? And how should we write it? There is more to it than one might think. Consider the following ways to use emotion in your prose.

Telling Emotions — Although it is always best to show emotion, there are times when it is appropriate to tell. For instance, if a character is describing another's emotion by saying, "Lucas was so excited by the results of his experiment," that is fine. After all, the character describing the other's emotion can only attest to what was seen and heard.

Showing Emotions — There are many ways to show emotion in your POV character. Using voice tone, body language, facial expressions, and physical and internal reactions helps your readers visualize and connect with the character. Let's examine the many ways to write realistic and compelling emotions in our prose.

External Emotions – Visual/Audible — Our facial expressions and body language are tattletales to our feelings and the feelings of others with whom we come in contact. Confusion may manifest with drawn eyebrows, the head tilted to one side, and arms crossed over the chest. Surprise is often manifested through arched eyebrows, jaw dropped open, maybe shoulders hunched over with hands covering the mouth. You can identify angry people across the room by hearing raised voices, arms flailing, hands pounding the table, hair falling onto their brows, getting into each other's personal space, and jabbing fingers in chests. No one has to tell you those people are angry. We see it, hear it.

Internal Emotions – We feel emotions without having to name them. The same should be true of our characters. Let's take the emotion of fear as an example. It causes our blood pressure to rise, our heart to beat wildly, and our breathing is shallow and rapid. Our stomachs may cramp, our bladders might leak, or we taste the salty bile that may rise in our throats. On the other hand, the emotion of peace causes our bodies to relax, our breathing to regulate and deepen.

Mental Emotions – Don't forget it isn't just our body that reacts to emotions, but our mental state is affected as well. Using fear as an example again, our mind races from one conclusion to the next. Our thoughts become muddled, and we can't make a decision. Whereas, when we are at peace, we not only think clearly, but we are also more creative and have greater insight.

EMOTION EXERCISE

Make an Emotion Thesaurus

The following is a list of some of the most common emotions. Either in a notebook or on a computer, give each emotion its own page and write the name of the emotion across the top. Next, divide the page into 5 sections and describe:
- Facial Expressions
- Gestures
- Body Language
- Physical reactions
- Psychological Reactions

Love	**Hate**
Happy	**Depressed**
Anger	**Doubt**
Excitement	**Fear**
Guilt	**Suspicion**
Frustration	**Impatience**
Compassion	**Annoyance**
Nervousness	**Confusion**
Contempt	**Eagerness**

Disgust	**Embarrassment**
Defeat	**Surprise**
Pride	**Resentment**
Worry	**Insecurity**
Hopefulness	**Hurt**
Jealousy	**Overwhelmed**
Reluctance	**Desire**
Desperation	**Envy**
Anticipation	**Shame**

NOTES

MEMOIR
WRITING LIFE BECAUSE YOUR STORY MATTERS

Our stories are one of the most important legacies we leave when we pass from this earth. ~ Linda Apple

In this chapter, I will continue to write about "story" only this time I will discuss true stories—to be exact, memoirs. There seems to be some confusion about what a memoir is and what it isn't. The word *memoir* comes from the French word *mémoire,* meaning memory or reminiscence. It is a retelling of moments, snapshots of life, written in rich detail.

Memoirs are sometimes confused with autobiographies, which are chronological. Someone once explained the difference by comparing an autobiography to a whole pie and memoirs to slices of pie—slices of life. Or think "snapshots" instead of the whole movie. The wonderful thing about writing memories is that you can write about many different things from life in a variety of formats, for instance, a cookbook with memories about recipes.

I had the privilege of meeting and befriending Walter "Boots" Mayberry. He was the grandfather to my son-in-law. Boots was a WWII POW. For years, he told stories to his family about the war. After hearing a few, I knew that as time went on and his stories were repeated by family members, they would be expanded and reshaped. His memories needed to be written to maintain their reliability. I volunteered to partner with him and write them just as he wanted them written. I interviewed him and listened to tapes he provided of his past interviews and noticed how some of his stories had already altered in his memory. We worked together. He dictated his memories to me. Then, I composed a chapter and gave him what I wrote for his approval. I think he saw how his stories were inflated and asked me to delete several scenes. When the manuscript was finished, I found a publisher for him. After the book was released, several of his family members were unhappy with it because it wasn't written in the way they remembered the retelling of his stories. But it was written how he wanted it.

Memories are a funny thing. They are not always 100% reliable. When we call on our brains to recall a memory, they are essentially reconstructed in our minds. While most of what we remember is true, many things come into play that interfere with complete accuracy.

One evening, when my adult children came over for supper, they reminisced about a family vacation at the beach. My husband and I remembered it as a complete disaster. None of them were happy. They whined and complained the entire time. But to hear them tell it, the trip was fantastic. It was interesting how they all gave different accounts of our trip. However, they all agreed that they loved it. *Huh?*

Speaking of different memories of the same thing, my son once told me how he remembered me using spoiled milk in their cereal. Let me just say, *I would NEVER do that, and I NEVER did.* But he insisted the milk was bad because it was curdled. Thinking back, I remembered how I used to buy several gallons of milk while I was in town because we lived thirty minutes from the closest store. I had five children, and we went through a gallon and a half a day. So, I kept some fresh and froze the others to keep them from spoiling before we used them. When I took the frozen milk from the freezer and put it in the refrigerator to thaw, I noticed how the cream came out in clumps. No amount of shaking would reincorporate it. It did look curdled, but I assure you it wasn't. So, in his reconstructed memory, he saw spoiled, curdled milk. In mine, I saw an efficient mom. It turned out that both of our memories of seeing what appeared to be curdled milk were correct. It came down to my son's perception.

Does this mean we shouldn't write our stories because they might contain some inaccuracies? Absolutely not. You write it as you remember it. After all, it is your story. Stick to it!

The greatest good will come from your stories when you are real in your writing. Be vulnerable, admit your quirks, weaknesses, and mistakes. Then, write how you overcame and what you learned. Readers need to know they are not alone, and there is hope.

WRITING A MEMOIR EXERCISE

So, where do you start when thinking about writing a memoir? Here are a few suggestions to get you started.

- Think about your purpose for writing a memoir. What is the message you want to impart, and how do you hope your readers will profit from your story?
- Choose suggestions from the following list and freewrite about each memory that comes to mind:
    - People who either inspired you or disheartened you and what you learned.
    - Your pets and what you learned from them.
    - Hobbies and interests
    - Your travels and how they impacted your view of life.
    - Living in another country
    - Songs, movies, authors, or books that inspired you.
    - Holidays and family traditions.
    - What your older self would tell your younger self.
    - Places you've lived.
    - School memories.
    - Jobs you've held.
    - What you've learned from nature.

- Spiritual and Religious experiences.
- Choices you've had to make between two great choices. Why did you choose what you did?
- The impact your grandparents had on you.
- Fresh starts and how they changed you.
- Historical events that have impacted you. Explain.

NOTES

Living through history — John W. Gardner, former United States Secretary of Health, Education, and Welfare, wrote, "History never looks like history when you are living through it." When I first read his quote, it was like a revelation. Since elementary school, I viewed history solely as occurrences that happened before I was born. I learned dates, facts, and figures, took the test, and forgot about it. To me, Pearl Harbor was black ink on a white page, with black and white photographs. As an adult, I never thought of events that happened in my lifetime as "history." Gardner's quote burst upon my consciousness and opened my eyes to the significance of historic occurrences about which I had personal knowledge. Students today are taught about 911, the Vietnam War, Neil Armstrong being the first man on the moon, and the assassination of President Kennedy—events that occurred before they were born. Merely presenting these as lessons filled with facts, figures, and photographs falls short, in my opinion. While the former is good and needful, I feel personal experiences linked to these occurrences are equally as important. I know the impact they had on me and how they contributed to who I am today.

My brother served two tours in Vietnam. We wrote back and forth, and I sent him pictures. Soon, his friends started writing me and asking for pictures. In fact, I was a pinup girl in his barracks.

They were that desperate, I suppose. I wore POW and MIA bracelets in honor of his comrades, hoping and praying for my brother to come home safely, as well as the men on my wrist. Only I can write about my emotional ties and thoughts about the Vietnam War, bringing the faces of the men and women into focus for my readers.

The lesson I learned from the September 11, 2001, attack is to not take anything for granted. Not to assume I had a tomorrow. Just think, who could have anticipated a jet crashing into their office? I thought about the unspoken sentiments—those "I love you," "Please forgive me," or "I forgive you," left hanging. How many people left for work after an argument, intending to reconcile later, only to have that chance taken away? I didn't want to be left with or leave that burden, and when I write about 9/11, it is with the hope that my readers will be inspired to take care of important matters right away.

LIVING THROUGH HISTORY EXERCISE

Just like before in the memoir exercise, choose from the list below and freewrite about where you were, how you were changed, lessons you learned, etc. This list to get you started, however, be sure and add to the list. A lot has happened in our lifetimes.
- The bombing of Pearl Harbor
- The assassination of John F Kennedy and Martin Luther King.
- Neil Armstrong walking on the moon.
- Passage of the Civil Rights Act.
- The Internet and personal home computers.
- Cell phones.
- The British music invasion, i.e., The Beetles.
- Elvis Presley
- Space Shuttle Challenger
- The 911 Attack
- President Barack Obama's election.
- Black Lives Matter
- COVID

NOTES

CREATIVE NONFICTION

We are members of the human family, and it is important to our development to understand where we came from, where we fit in, and learn the same about other cultures as well. By writing our stories we give the gift of connection—a gift that transcends time and enrichs the lives of our readers.

There are many reasons people want to write about their lives. I write to inspire others to a more fulfilling life. After all, in this troubled world, it is easy to feel powerless to do anything to make things better. In this chapter, I hope to remind you of the power you have in your words and in your stories. Mark Twain once said, "A drop of ink may make millions think." To inspire, encourage, and help others, even if it is just one person, starts a ripple effect on everyone in the scope of that one person. Also, *how* you write is key to powerful stories. Using the Creative Nonfiction technique will connect your reader with your writing because you are using fiction techniques to tell the truth.

What Creative Nonfiction is – Lee Gutkind, called "the Godfather" behind this genre, is the leading figure behind the creative nonfiction movement and the first to use the term "creative nonfiction." Universities resisted his suggestion that CNF be included as a writing course, including the university where he taught. However, he worked tirelessly to bring legitimacy to this genre because he wanted students to connect with the real world through what he called "the literature of reality." He describes CNF as "true stories, well told." Nonfiction stories well told are written with fiction techniques. Creative Nonfiction stories are true, the characters are real, and the facts are accurate, period.

Whether you are writing literary or personal narrative nonfiction, journalism, essays, or memoirs, you will include plot, scenes, a story arc, a sense of place, dialogue, internalization, and emotion, as discussed earlier. Hopefully, you will also add a personal reflection—a powerful gift you give your reader.

What Creative Nonfiction is Not—There is a lot of confusion about CNF. Creative does not mean you can invent what didn't happen, add characters who were not there, combine characters into one, or describe what wasn't there. Creative doesn't mean a license to lie.

As I mentioned at the beginning of this chapter, we all "misremember" some things. In those cases, we can only write as we remember, being as honest as we can. Dialogue also presents a problem for CNF purists. Personally, I cannot remember word-for-word what I said an hour ago. But I have a good idea about what was said. If we do not change the facts and keep to the gist of a conversation, we are fine. I usually qualify by writing; *I remember she said something like..."* That said, there are two instances where the dialogue you write MUST be verbatim: when quoting someone or when replicating text from another source.

When writers make stuff up to beef up their nonfiction, it moves into the category of "faction" fiction based on fact.

CNF Personal Reflection— This is important when using creative nonfiction when writing either personal experience stories or true inspirational essays. We give our readers something to encourage them and perhaps apply to their own lives. When writing my reflection, I avoid *the moral of the story* tone. It is important never to tell your reader how to think. This is especially true for devotions, inspirational and spiritual pieces. I've often found when judging contests in these categories that many of the entries were either teachy, preachy or to a point, condescending.

To inspire others through personal experience and observations is to be vulnerable, open, and honest. It is mentoring, assuring your reader you've been there, done that, and got the t-shirt. Your observations should lift up your readers by helping them observe from a higher and more hopeful viewpoint.

Furthermore

Never Stop Learning. Always be Teachable

Michelle Obama said, "We should always have three friends in our lives. One who walks ahead, who we look up to and follow. One who walks beside us, who is with us every step of our journey, and then, one who we reach back for and bring along after we've cleared the way."

This is true for every writer. I had the privilege of having two excellent mentors, Dusty Richards and Velda Brotherton, who walked ahead of me and reached back for me, having cleared the way. But it was Dusty who drilled us on the writerly rules every week during critique group.

A bear of a man, Dusty wrote 170 Westerns and traveled the nation teaching about writing. Dusty was one of the best advocates a writer could have. The tips from Dusty that I'm going to share offer valuable guidance, but they aren't strict rules set in stone. While others may present them as rigid rules, I've found that it is okay to break some rules after you learn them. Following Dusty's advice will make your writing shine. However, if you find your sentence is too convoluted to keep within the rules, go ahead and break them...occasionally.

Dusty's Advice
- Avoid over-using "to be" verbs. To-be verbs include words am, are, is, was, were, be, being, and been. All these words are sometimes necessary for clarity. However, when you can, choose to use active voice instead. For example, instead of writing, *The cat was being chased by the dog,* Write, *The dog chased the cat.* Instead of, *Marsha was sad,* write, *Marsha wiped a tear from her eye.* Both examples using "was" puts the character in a "static" state. It is better to show action. Which shows a more vivid picture: *Neal was in his chair,* or *Neal slumped in his chair?* The first example is a state of being. The second shows us Neal in his chair and his emotion.
- Do not overuse adverbs. Those "ly" words tell the reader instead of showing. Instead of, *She angrily walked away.* Say, *She swung fisted hands and strode away.* When you can use an action verb, do it. Also, as mentioned earlier in this book, avoid using adverbs as dialogue tags.

- Watch for redundant words. I'm as guilty as the next person of using these words. Examples are: sit down—sitting already suggests down. Stand up already suggests up. Additional phrases are actual fact, join together, unexpected surprise, end result, and the list goes on. See how each implies the same thing?
- Avoid excessive use of dialogue tags. When there are only two people in a scene, there is no need to use a dialogue tag after each sentence. Instead, start a new paragraph after each character speaks. The reader knows who is speaking by the formatting. I will also mention one of my pet peeves here. When there is only one character in the scene, after introducing the character's name at the beginning of the scene, there is no reason to keep repeating his or her name.
- No *prairie dogs*! This was Dusty's word for repetitive words. We all have them in our writing. In recent books I've read, one book mentioned "thighs" on every other page. Another author repeatedly used the word "circle." One author constantly mentioned a "fishtail braid." My word is "just." Believe me, before this book is published I will do a search to get rid of most of them. But you will probably identify more.
- Don't begin every sentence with a noun/verb. For example:

He walked into the room.
She dropped her glass when she saw him.
He hurried to her, "Did I startle you?"
She shook her head. "No, I was just surprised."
He smiled. "Good, that is what I hoped for."

Do you see the noun/verb pattern? *He walked, She dropped, He hurried, She shook, He smiled.*

Instead, write the scene something like this:

She dropped her glass when he walked into the room.

"Did I startle you?"

"No." She bent and picked up her glass. "I was just surprised."

"Good." He smiled. "That is what I hoped for."

- Finally, he advised us to get a great editor. Not your mom, not your best friend, but someone who will be honest and thorough. I won't lie, it is hard to hear anyone criticize your work even when you've asked for it and they have the best intentions. But this step is necessary for the excellence of your work.

THE END...OR IS IT?

"... the first draft is the down draft – you just get it down. The second draft is the up draft – you fix it up." ~ Anne Lamott

After you've written your story or book and you type those blessed words, "The End." It really isn't. Your writing journey is far from over. You've just written your first draft. You've told yourself the story. You've written down the bones. The second draft is fleshing out the bones. You ensure the story flows, check for holes, improve imagery, use stronger words. The third draft is where you cut unnecessary things. Here you will need an editor for content and grammar. By now you will be too close to your story and will see everything as imperative. An editor will be objective. In the fourth draft you will incorporate the editor's suggestions and make sure your manuscript is clean and ready. Honestly, you could continually rewrite drafts, but at some point you must let it go.

The elements I've shared in this book are something every story needs, but there are also fundamentals that are not mentioned. Each genre' has its own unique nuance. I encourage you to research your genre online, find a critique group, and attend writer conferences. You will find wide and varied opinions, and here is where you must choose what resonates with you. When you listen to critiques in writer groups or speakers at a conference, you will often hear conflicting advice. Apart from the basics on these pages, the opinions will greatly vary. The same is true for publishers. They have their own set of rules, and it is wise to follow their guidelines.

The most important advice I can give, however, is for you to trust yourself and write. Get your stories down. As the quote suggests, you can fix it up later.

Anne Lamott wrote, *"We are not here to see through one another, but to see one another through."*. No matter what genre you write in, if you write from your "Dash," you will not only help see others through, but you will also leave a great legacy for the generations who come after you.

Your stories matter. Write!

ABOUT THE AUTHOR

Acclaimed author and motivational speaker Linda Apple writes inspirational nonfiction, women's fiction, and books for children featuring her Scottish terrier, Winston.

Her first book about Winston was on the shortlist for the Benjamin Franklin Award. Public schools have used her Winston chapter book series, which features Social and Emotional Learning, for their One Book programs. Linda enjoys visiting schools and speaking to all of Winston's fans. His newest book *ARF! Winston's Arfsome Real-life Fables* is now available.

Linda has served as the president of the Oklahoma Writers Federation, Inc. and the Ozark Creative Writers Conference. She also has the great honor of being chosen to be inducted into the 2023 Arkansas Writers Hall of Fame. Linda has taught writing workshops nationally and internationally.

She is a firm believer in writing with her readers in mind and leaving them better after having read her books. She also encourages writers and readers alike to value their own stories and to share them. She aims to spread seeds of inspiration and give wings to all she has the privilege to mentor. She writes from her soul and speaks from her heart.

Linda lives in Northwest Arkansas with her husband, children, fourteen grandchildren, and her writing partner, Winston, a feisty Scottish Terrier. He barks; she types.

www.ingramcontent.com/pod-product-compliance
Lightning Source LLC
Chambersburg PA
CBHW071306040426
42444CB00009B/1888